"The Business Leaders Essential Guide to Growth"

How to grow your business with confidence, control, and reward.

Eliminate the barriers to growth and never look back.

Stephen Dann

Published in the United Kingdom by Business Impact Solutions Ltd

Book design & layout by Velin@Perseus-Design.com

Email: bisbooks@businessimpactsolutions.co.uk
Website: www.businessimpactsolutions.co.uk

ISBN: 978-1-7399798-0-5

First Edition

The Business Leaders Essential Guide to Growth

Businesses rarely seem to grow quite in the way their owners want them to. They either grow too fast or too slow or not at all. Sometimes they even go backwards.

Every successful business has experienced each one of the following stages. They can go from achieving amazing results and lofty goals to the brutal reality of fighting for survival.

Whatever stage you are at, achieving consistent sustainable growth presents a wide range of problems and challenges. These must be overcome to enable the business to progress - ignoring them will stop you achieving your ambitions and make decline inevitable.

In *The Business Leaders Essential Guide to Growth*, renowned business adviser, Stephen Dann sets out the methods, the tools, and the techniques to enable your business to develop, thrive and grow. so, you can achieve your business and personal goals.

Whether you are a business owner, director, or entrepreneur, *The Business Leaders Essential Guide to Growth* enables you to eliminate the barriers to growth and build your business with confidence, control, and reward.

You discover:

- How to gain clarity on your current situation
- How to build, manage and motivate your teams
- How your key business drivers fit together
- Where to focus and what to measure
- The process to ensure your plans are implemented
- What's going to get in your way

I wish you success in your journey.

Acknowledgements

Inevitably there are too many people to thank as in reality every single person I've worked with, every book I've read and every business experience I've had have all contributed to this book.

But specific thanks should go to:

Peter Thomson for writing the foreword and for providing the impetus to get these books out of my head and onto the page. I know I would not have written 1 book (certainly not a series of books) without the advice, ideas and stimulation of Peter and his team.

Christopher Bayliss for his inspiration and energy, for proving the power of peer group learning, and showing that the "answer is always in the room".

Finally, the many clients who have trusted me to help, guide, support and push them along their growth journeys. Working with them reminds me that every day is a learning day and a constant reminder that building and growing a business is tough, challenging, exhilarating, exasperating, satisfying, and rewarding - often in the same day.

Foreword

At age 21, my then sales manager told me, "If you don't know where you're going, all the roads lead there!". That was the prompt for me to set goals. A practice I've kept to this day.

If only I had also known Stephen Dann on the day I started my first business all those years ago. The heartaches, the money, the effort he could have saved me by making me aware of the questions I needed to ask myself. And the questions I needed to ask of others: colleagues, customers, and suppliers.

For the current and future generations of business leaders and entrepreneurs, they no longer must suffer as I did. They have Stephen Dann. They have his experience, his expertise, his insights (and most importantly) his questions.

You are holding in your hand – a proven process to take your business (regardless of sector) and make it the success it surely deserves to be.

Each chapter clearly explains the why, the what and the how. It poses the questions that must be answered by any business leader who's hungry for success for his business, his people and himself.

The inspirational effect of these questions mustn't be overlooked. Just by reading them one feels more focused, more alive to possibilities and more ready to take action.

Seldom has such a short book in size been so long in instantly useable content.

On behalf of the business community and entrepreneurs everywhere, – "Thank you Stephen"

Peter Thomson

"The UK's Most Prolific `Information Product Creator"
www.peterthomson.com

Introduction

Let's be honest ...

You have chosen a tough challenge. One which will constantly stretch your capabilities and expose you to both the exhilaration of success and the terror of failure. Sometimes in the same day.

Growing a business takes considerable time, focus and effort. No one else can do it but you. Maybe you have a great team to help, but it is only you who can inspire, manage, and guide them.

Great businesses often falter when it comes to implementation and follow through. So, I cannot guarantee complete success.

But I can show you the methods, the tools, and the techniques I have learned through deep experience. I can set out the ways to enable your business to develop, thrive and grow to achieve your goals and ambitions.

Developing and growing a business will require you to consistently master new disciplines and skills. You are certainly going to need to find more customers, innovate and think differently at every stage of the journey.

Innovation and marketing are the subjects of two further books in this series. In this one we will concentrate on the tools and techniques that enable you to grow your business and be in control of that growth.

Having built my own businesses and worked with over 400 entrepreneurs I have been able to identify and distil the key strands that are necessary for success

I've also, both from first-hand experience and experience of others, learned from the lessons of failure. It is often said that we learn more from our failures than from our successes.

Whether you are growing too fast, too slow, or not at all, it is my hope that by the time you have finished this book you will be primed for success. You will be confident that you really can grow your business, be fully in control of the process and reap the rewards.

Table of Contents

THE BASIC STRATEGIC QUESTIONS

"IF YOU DON'T KNOW WHERE YOU ARE GOING, ALL ROADS LEAD THERE"

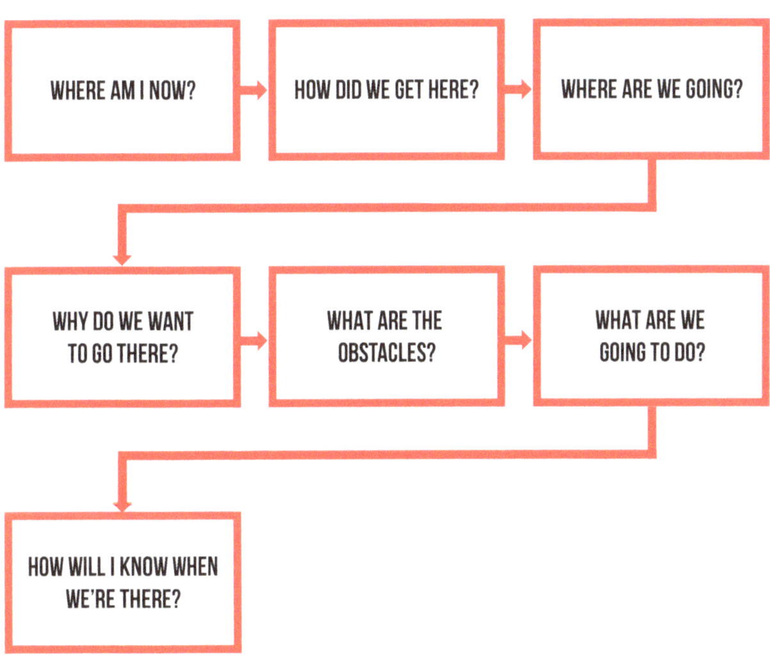

1.

Where are you now?

Every journey has a starting point and a destination, a beginning, and an end. So, before we can build the route map, we need to be clear, and if need be, brutally honest, about the starting point.

So, let us start by defining the reality of your business today. (I will use the word "business" throughout this series of books, but this could be any organisation, charity, division, team or a specific product or service).

Clarity on the current situation of the business will be fundamental to developing your growth plans. This section covers a selection of ways to define the situation today and to focus on the critical ones. So, grab a notebook and let's sketch out how your business looks today:

Describe your business:

Imagine you are talking openly and honestly to a friend (not a potential customer or your bank manager).

What is it that your company or product does?

What is the background or history?

What has the journey been like so far?

What does it really feel like to be working in your business today?

Ask your team to complete the same exercise - this should be done 'top of the head', not copied from the website, nor from an existing plan or brochure - so that you are able to capture exact words and understanding. You may well find that your team struggles to articulate the essence of the business, does it differently to you or inconsistently.

It is also worth asking your customers too, as their perspective may well be quite different to your own.

Telephone your top 10 customers and ask them these two simple questions:

a) what do we do for you?

b) why do you choose us?

BACKGROUND / HISTORY

BACKGROUND AND HISTORY

WHAT IS IT THAT YOUR COMPANY OR PRODUCT DOES?

WHAT IS THE BACKGROUND OR HISTORY?

WHAT HAS THE JOURNEY BEEN LIKE SO FAR?

Then write down the exact words that they use - you may be surprised that both the perceptions and language used by customers will be significantly different to those used inside the business.

From this you will have three different perspectives - your own, your team's and your customers'. If you are to grow, then there is the critical fourth perspective of your prospective customers who may not even be aware of you yet or may have already formed an opinion.

PERSPECTIVES

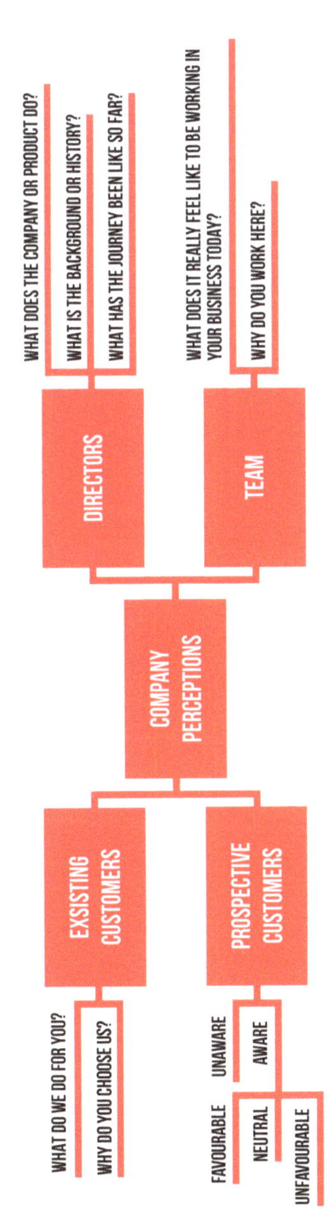

OTSW Analysis

I am sure everyone is familiar with SWOT analysis. Many plans contain extensive lists of strengths, weaknesses, opportunities, and threats. Quite how these are all turned into specific actions is often unclear.

If your purpose is to develop and grow your business and put it on a different trajectory then a combination of focus and change will be essential. Growth will come from focusing mindset and efforts on to opportunities. Therefore, we need to change the order and whilst OTSW does not have the memorability of SWOT it does help focus on what really matters.

Opportunities and threats are external to the business and outside of your control.

Strengths and weaknesses are internal to the business and within your control.

So:

What are the key **Opportunities** in the market?

What are the key external **Threats** that may disrupt you?

What are the internal **Strengths** already in the business that will help you with the market opportunity?

OTSW

OPPORTUNITIES (MARKET & EXTERNAL)	THREATS (MARKET & EXTERNAL)
STRENGTHS (BUSINESS & INTERNAL)	WEAKNESSES (BUSINESS & INTERNAL)

What are the internal **Weaknesses** that must be resolved to enable you to capitalise on the opportunity?

Be as specific as possible in defining the opportunities in the marketplace.

Having analysed this, you may find that you lack significant scope or scale of opportunities which would be a valuable conclusion.

Who are you up against?

So now let us think about competitors.

Unfortunately, you are not alone in the marketplace. Existing competitors will be vying for the same customers and new competitors may well be just over the horizon.

Who is fighting with you for the same customer?

Who is providing an alternative solution to your customer's problem?

Write a list of key competitors. Against each, list their strengths and most importantly their weaknesses. We naturally overplay competitors' strengths, believe their marketing claims, and can become discouraged. Customers however are adept at uncovering weaknesses - and through social media and review platforms are happy to share their experience. Focus on your competitors' weaknesses, not their strengths.

(Tip: if your competitors use review platforms such as Trustpilot, Google or Facebook, check out their negative reviews to see what customers really care about.)

COMPETITORS

WHO ARE YOU UP AGAINST?
THESE CAN BE SPECIFIC COMPANIES, PRODUCTS, OR CATEGORIES OF COMPETITOR AS WELL AS ALTERNATIVE WAYS THAT CLIENTS HAVE OF FULFILLING THE NEED:

WHO/WHAT?
THEIR STRENGTHS?
THEIR WEAKNESSES?

What does a current good customer look like?

If you want to achieve growth in future it will most likely come by targeting similar types of customers with similar values and problems. To do this we need to take a reality check on your current customers:

List your top 10 customers:

They should be the ones that are most important to you in terms of revenue, fit and longevity. What is their profile? How did you find them?

For B2B, note down the sector or industry, the job role of your key contact, job role of any other influencer or decision maker.

List your last 10 lost customers:

Why did you lose them? Where did they go? How were they different from your top 10 customers?

List your most recent 10 lost potential sales:

Why didn't you get the order? Were they wrong fit customers? Where did they go?

Know your numbers

Keeping aware of the basic metrics which drive any business can really help expose flaws, show where improvement can easily stimulate growth and help define the scale of the journey ahead:

Retention Rate

What percentage of your customers do you keep from 1 year to the next?

Lifetime Value

What is the total value of a customer to you throughout the entire period in which they are a customer?

Repeat rate

How often do customers reorder?

Conversion model

How many leads or enquiries do you need to get one new customer?

Where are you on your growth journey?

On the journey from start-up to global corporate, businesses must navigate many different phases and challenges. This journey is never a straight line or straight forward with each growth phase having periods of stability, evolution, reinvention, and change. To get from one stage to the next, significant barriers must be overcome - however it is the role of the business leader which must change the most.

In the early phase communication is easy, with maybe everyone working in the same office, so everyone knows what is going on. Your early-stage team is likely to be comfortable with fluidity, energy, and informality. But, by the time you get to 50 (or 150) people in multiple offices (in multiple countries) the challenges are completely different.

It is also likely that your early team may no longer be the right team for the next stage of your journey. You will now need rules, procedures, policies, HR, and reports which starts to feel rather corporate and less entrepreneurial. There may even become the point where you are no longer the right person to run your own business.

Rest assured that the crisis points on the growth journey are normal. Businesses that stagnate simply fail to (or do not wish to) break through to the next stage. In assessing the current situation, do not forget to look at your own role too and reflect on whether it's time to rethink your own job description.

GREINER'S GROWTH CURVE

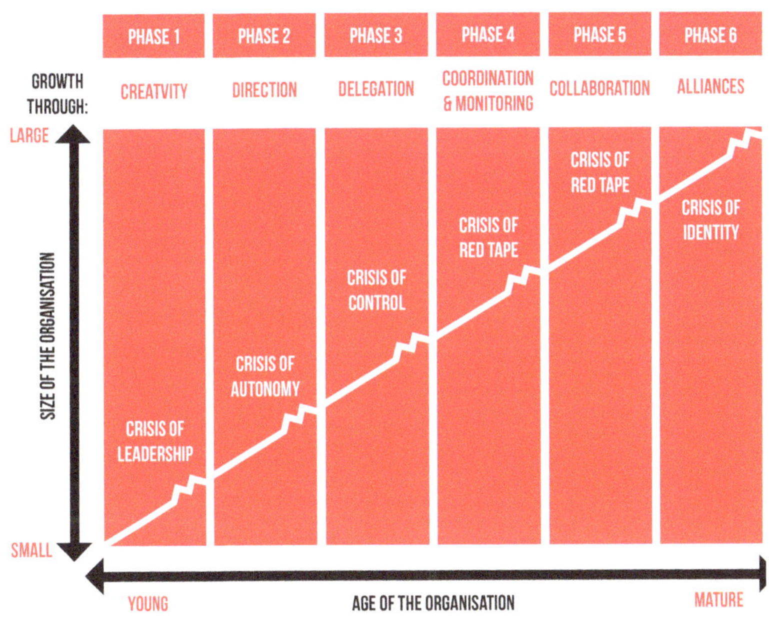

(*THE MODEL WAS CREATED BY LARRY GREINER IN 1972 AND UPDATED IN 1998*)

What are your conclusions?

Hopefully, you now have a substantive view of the current situation, but like most situation analyses it may be easy to think, "so what?" If we are to move this from just being "interesting", we need to narrow down the focus onto a short list of key issues to be resolved. The rest of your analysis remains totally valid. But we must prioritise to ensure that the plan is deliverable and within the time and resources available. Better by far to succeed in nailing a few issues rather than not finish many.

So, what are your key conclusions?

What insights are there?

What gaps in information or knowledge are there?

Which are the key challenges which your plans must resolve?

What really must change?

Further on in this book, these will form the basis of your Growth Goals and Priority Plans – the key problems and challenges which need to be tackled.

KEY ISSUES

WHAT ARE THE CONCLUSIONS FROM THE SITUATION ANALYSIS?

2.

What do you believe in?

Ever since Simon Sinek made his famous TED talk on company purpose in 2010, we have become perhaps too obsessed with establishing a higher purpose for businesses on the assumption that customers and employees will flock to you accordingly. But this is not a quick fix - in the same way that vision statements and mission statements can become bland and meaningless. Simply bolting on a "save the planet" type purpose or jumping on the latest fashionable bandwagon fools no one." Purpose-washing" is not the solution.

To be credible, your driving force must be genuine, authentic, honest, and believable. It needs to set you apart from your competitors, motivate your customers and energise your teams too.

Most companies talk a lot about what they do and how they do it (i.e. their products). But customers today are also concerned with the nature of the company that sits behind a product or service. They do not just want a great product. The same applies to your team also.

A framework which defines the purpose and principles by which you operate will help underpin key decisions. It will provide guidance to your teams and customers on how they should expect the business to behave.

Do remember that "making money" is not a purpose. It is the outcome or result at the end of the process. So:

Why?

Why do you exist? Why do you do what you do? What is the purpose of your company? What are you passionate about? In what ways do you make a difference? What do you really believe in or care about? Why would customers care if they could no longer buy your product?

How?

How do you do what you do for your customers? How is this unique?

What?

What are the specific things you do for your customers? What do they achieve from this? What impact does this have on them?

Results?

What benefits or outcomes do you receive as a result?

Overall, what are the guiding principles for your business which will ensure your teams always perform at their best, work smoothly together, and deliver outstanding service to customers who will enthusiastically reorder, endorse and recommend?

No matter how virtuous your purpose, it does need to match the reality of your business and all its practices. This means that all your business functions, departments and teams need to understand the company purpose, vision and values and ensure they always fulfil them.

Businesses with purpose, grow faster and retain staff better.

PURPOSE PYRAMID

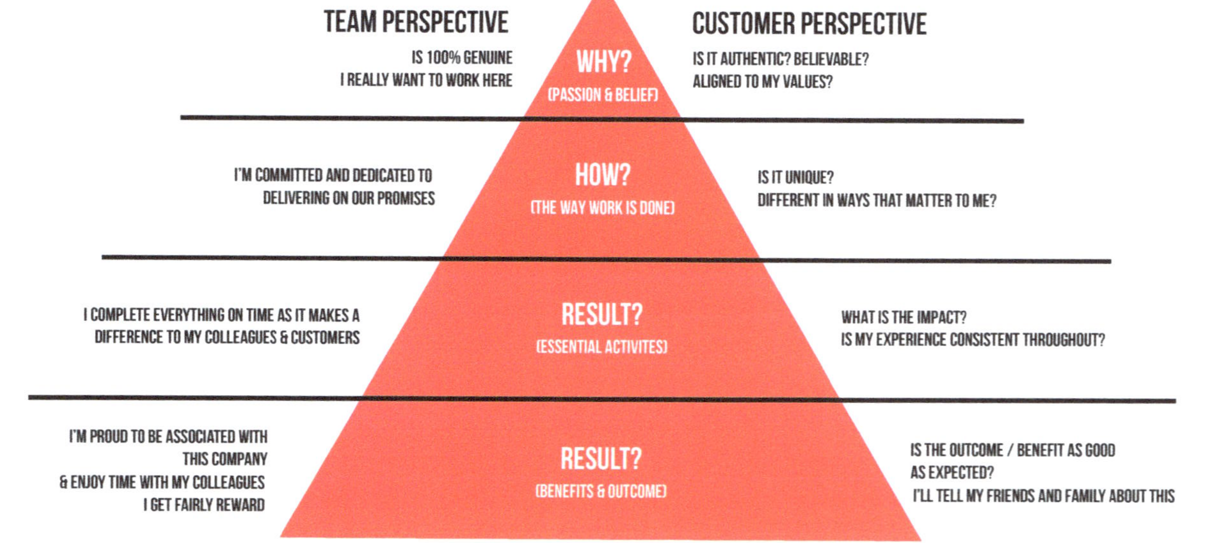

3.

How do you want your teams to behave?

For many, this is the toughest part of growing a business. Certainly, if you are to grow, then you and your teams will have to get used to a process of constant change and evolution. Roles and responsibilities of team members need to develop as the scale and needs of the business changes. This may require recruiting different team members with specific expertise, behaviours, and values. It is unlikely that the team that got you to where you are today will get you to where you want to be in the future.

It's a bit like a relay race, with the baton passing on repeatedly to get to the next stage. However, there are multiple relay races running in parallel in each of your business functions. There are always more stages and the finishing line is forever moving too.

So, what are the key areas to focus on?

"In vs Out" Behaviours

Firstly let's establish the key behaviours, values, and standards. These will underpin your teams to ensure that they are working in a way that is most appropriate for your business. To do this we need to list the behaviours which belong in the team and are fundamental to successful outcomes. We also need to list the behaviours that do not belong in the team which will fundamentally lead to failure. By defining these you will have both a "success blueprint" and a "failure blueprint". It's a good idea to involve the team in this process to enable them to identify what represents good behaviour (In – "Our Way") and bad behaviour (Out – "Not Our Way"). The final list should be publicly visible and can be added to and modified, as necessary.

On a regular basis discuss with the team what the key enablers and blockers are which will help them or prevent them from adhering to these behaviour standards and obstruct achieving the outcomes. Using this approach your team are empowered to call out anyone who is not adhering to these behaviour standards - including you. If the wrong behaviours are tolerated, they quickly become accepted and normal. Sometimes it's the business owner or managing director who is the biggest rule breaker and the most disruptive person in the business!

WHAT BEHAVIOURS, VALUES & STANDARDS WILL UNDERPIN SUCCESS?

IN (DESIRABLE BEHAVIOURS)	OUT (UNDESIRABLE BEHAVIOURS)

Goals

A team without clear agreed goals is impossible to manage or motivate. So, it is critical that every team member (including yourself) has clear goals and these are shared and visible. Complete transparency of goals at every level, from top to bottom is essential to ensure everyone can contribute fully and help develop a collaborative culture.

Goals are best planned together, defined briefly and clearly, and show what good performance looks like. They should be quantified and have specific dates for completion. Thereafter review the most important goals frequently and prompt your team to check if their behaviour is aligned to achieving their goals. (Tip: Read "The One Minute Manager" by Ken Blanchard & Spencer Johnson to remind yourself of the importance of basing your team interaction around their goals, and how to respond when they achieve or fail).

OKRs

One of the simplest and most powerful approaches to goal setting is the "OKR".

"OKRs have helped lead us to 10x growth, many times over. They have helped make our crazily bold mission of 'organizing the world's information' perhaps even achievable. They've kept me and the rest of the company on time and on track when it mattered the most" Larry Page, CEO of Alphabet and co-founder of Google.

Originally used at Intel, OKRs quickly became part of Google's culture as a management methodology to help ensure that the company focuses efforts on the same important issues throughout the organization.

OKRs comprise an **O**bjective (a clearly defined goal) and several **K**ey **R**esults (specific measures used to track the achievement of that goal).

The key result must be measurable, so at the end you can without any debate tell if it was done or not. No arguments, discussion, or judgements: Did I do that, or did I not do it? Yes? No?

The OKR Blueprint:

Objectives.

Define 3-5 key objectives on company, team, or personal levels.

Objectives should be Inspiring, Difficult, Explicit, Achievable

They can be "Committed" or "Aspirational"

Key Results.

For each objective, define 3-5 measurable results.

Key results should be Specific, Measurable, Achievable, Relevant, Timebound, but not impossible.

OKR results could be based on growth, performance, revenue, or engagement.

Often, they are numerical, but they can also show if something is done or not done.

Publish & Share.

Ensure **all** OKRs are visible for **everyone** to see
(Tip: it's particularly important that the directors OKRs are visible)

OKR TEMPLATE

OBJECTIVE	WHAT DO YOU AIM TO ACHIEVE? WHAT IS THE GOAL?

- IS IT INSPIRING, DIFFICULT, EXPLICIT, ACHIEVABLE?
- IS IT COMMITTED (GUARANTEED) OR ASPIRATIONAL (STRETCHING)?
- IS IT PERSONAL, TEAM OR COMPANY GOAL?

TO:

KEY RESULTS	HOW WILL YOU DO THIS?	HOW WILL YOU KNOW YOU HAVE ACHIEVED IT?

- SPECIFIC, MEASURABLE, ACHIEVABLE, RELEVANT, TIMEBOUND

'AS MEASURED BY...'

1

2

3

4

5

Bold Motivating Goals

Goals need to be motivating for the company, the management, the teams, and the individuals - motivation can be both personal & financial. Having a goal to be the market leader sounds good, but what would this look like? What would it mean at an individual level? Why would this motivate? "What's in it for me?" ...

Remember not everyone wants to grow and conquer the world. Some may be comfortable where they are. They may not understand or know how to. They may even be frightened by your plans. They may need encouragement and motivating - they may also need to be convinced and believe you are up to it as well!

Barriers and constraints

Fast growing businesses can sometimes be constrained by a lack of belief that the growth goal is achievable, or a lack of desire to put the effort in. As a result, the team may appear slow to act and low on initiative. Remember that in most situations, 15% of people will be with you, 15% will be against you, 70% will be open to persuasion.

On occasions, people just do not know what to do or how to do it. So if a lack of skills or experience is holding them back (and sometimes fear of owning up to it) then appropriate training, can boost self-belief and performance considerably. This should be backed up by ongoing support (coaching or mentoring). Sales teams need to be regularly re-familiarised with the key benefits of the business to maintain a "superior value added" rather than "transactional" approach. Often a weekly training session (sales skill + technical knowledge) before or after hours works well.

There can be genuine constraints which hold teams back - system flaws, cumbersome or unnecessary processes, lack of knowledge or experience, inadequate resources, or information. Streamlining processes, eliminating wasted time, and automating tedious tasks can have a significant impact on performance and attitude. The simple question "what's holding you back from 100% growth / increase / output?" can be revealing - the best person to own the fix to the issue is of course the person who identified it.

Leadership

The business leader and the senior management team sets the tone. So, they must project consistent ambition, drive, energy, serious intent, and total belief in the team. The vision and values need to be articulated and most importantly owned and lived by the whole business. They should be fundamental to all induction, prominently displayed and regularly reinforced. All plans and actions should be referenced against them.

Motivation (RAMP)

This is a complex subject and there are many excellent models which help explain what causes individuals to act and behave in certain ways. There is no one size fits all. You will need to motivate your team on an individual basis; however, the following general motivator principles may help:

Relationships

To be recognised for what they do. To work with and relate to other team members, belong to a community, help others improve, use their mind and experience fully.

Autonomy

To self-manage, freedom to be flexible, work their own way, add personal flair, work on their own and part of a team.

Mastery

To learn new skills, professional development, widen experience.

Purpose

To know the purpose of the business and how their role contributes. Do something bigger than themselves, social contribution, helping others.

Primary Motivating Factors (PMF)

One of the strongest ways to create loyal high performing teams is to recognise everyone's primary motivating factor. If you can understand your team members' dreams, ambitions, and wants; then aligning their work to help them achieve them is clearly beneficial for both sides. It is worth remembering that the primary motivating factors below may change over time:

- Extra Income
- Financial Freedom
- Have own business
- More spare time
- Personal development
- Helping Others
- Meeting new people
- Retirement
- Leaving a legacy

Values v Performance

Typically, when the need for recruitment arises it is because a specific skills gap has been identified. The job specification is drafted detailing the level of skill, the qualifications and level of experience required. Equally typically the "hot shot" candidate proves to be an expensive and disruptive failure. After six months of frustration and disappointment you may discover that you already have a junior member of the team who with the right level of training, support and encouragement can step up.

So why does this happen? Simply it's because we fall into the trap of recruiting for performance rather than values. Every time, you will achieve a better result by recruiting people who align with your values and the way you work. Business owners often say they want to find people who "just get it" but struggle to define what "it" actually is. "It" relates to your values and behaviours; the DNA of your business, what makes it different, special and a great place to work. By focussing on your values, you are more likely to attract people who may also have the performance and skills you need.

PERFORMANCE V VALUES

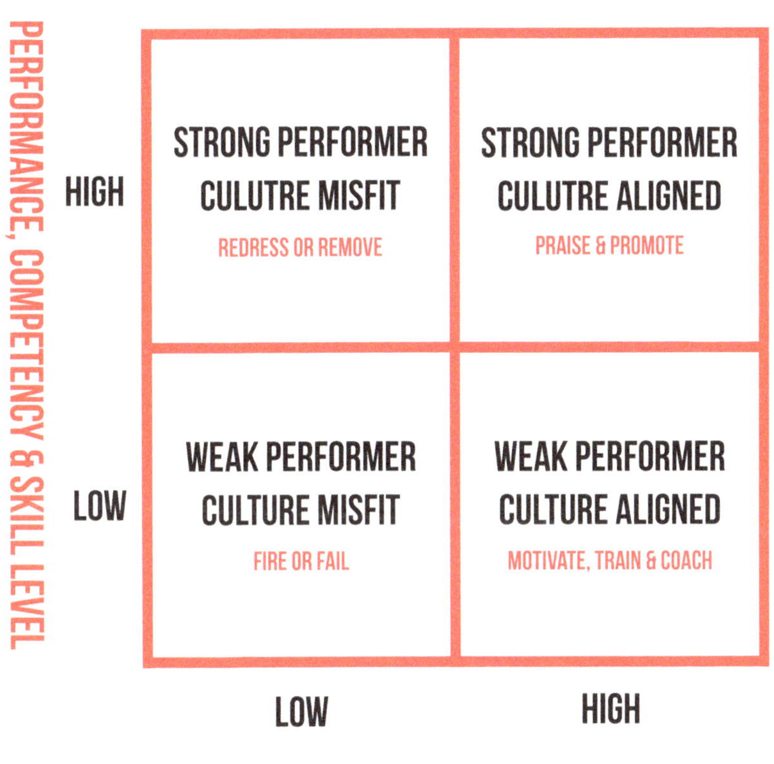

Recruit slowly

Recruitment is far from an exact science and success rates vary. But a failed hire is an expensive mistake, in terms of the cost, time invested and disruption. There is always the temptation to appoint someone into a role and "hope they come right" simply because the gap is causing pressure. Please resist and take your time. Hiring the right person 3 months later is vastly better than hiring the wrong person today. Remember that, change is unsettling for your existing team too and they often assume the new hires are getting a better deal.

The other frequent flaw in recruiting, is hiring people exactly like yourself. An effective balanced team needs a good variety of personality types.

Onboarding

Apart from the values misfit, the other main reason new hires do not fulfil expectations is due to weak on-boarding. It is easy to assume they will just get stuck in and use their experience to figure it out. On the contrary it takes a lot of effort to successfully bring someone new on board. So, before they start there needs to be a detailed onboarding plan covering the first 3 months with specific review points to check on progress. The goal must be to get the new hire up to speed and productive as fast as possible; it will not happen naturally by some sort of osmosis. Also, do not forget that the next generation is different to yours. They may have different ideas on work practices, values, priorities, loyalties, communication tools, attitudes, aspiration, and behaviours.

Job Descriptions & Reviews

Everyone needs a brief job description which sets out the purpose of the role, key responsibilities, and tasks (Tip: you should have one too). Quarterly reviews and appraisals are an ideal way of keeping the team on track, checking on progress and assisting with any log jams. If you don't want to go as far as a formal appraisal process, just use the job description as a checklist to discuss. You may well find it needs updating to reflect the changed reality of the role. Your teams need clarity of expectations and feedback.

The challenge of fast-growing businesses is that every job role must change too to keep in pace. If you grow by 100%, every function will have to cope with twice as much work. Not surprisingly team members may not be quite as enthusiastic about your growth journey if all it means is excessive workloads and hassle. It is crucial to allay these fears and reassure them that you will be recruiting and investing in technology to ensure they are not overloaded and have fulfilling roles. A regular review and reallocation of roles and responsibilities is essential to ensure the team can deliver.

Assuming you have recruited people who enjoy change, fluidity, and new challenges it provides the opportunity for them to reinvent their roles, responsibilities and learn new skills on a regular basis. Even in major corporates, some have a policy of job rotation to ensure their teams stay fresh, build skills and understanding.

Actions speak louder than words

It was our fourth meeting to set out plans to develop a green sustainable agenda. So far, we had worked on customers, manufacturing, and suppliers. My client was serious about sustainability. Now it was time to focus on the internal dimension, how to get the team to buy into sustainability.

"The trouble is, they just do not seem to get it", said the CEO. "I know that many of our team take green and sustainable issues seriously in their private lives, but it all seems to go out of the window when they come to work"

We discussed this for some time, coming up with a range of ideas to try and align behaviour better with the company goal. Then I asked, "So what do people get fired for around here? Do people get fired for not hitting the numbers or not following the sustainability policy?" Quick as a flash came the reply, "We have to deliver on our forecast, so missing sales and financial performance targets are not an option".

So, no surprise that his team will never embrace sustainability. It is simply a distraction, a barrier, a nuisance and getting in the way of them delivering what he really wants. Frankly so long as they hit their numbers, they will not care how they do It - that is what the CEO's actual behaviour is telling them. In this case, if sustainability is fundamental to competitive advantage, then it must be acceptable to miss the numbers because the business (the board, shareholders etc) believes a sustainable strategy will win.

It's easy to speak the words of "growth" and "high performance". But if actual management behaviour and team experience does not reflect this, then people will follow the behaviour they experience in practise. If the ambition to grow conflicts with the everyday reality of needing to hit short term sales targets, then people will focus on the short-term sales targets.

As leaders, you get the behaviour that you reward and that you exhibit yourself. Your team will ultimately follow what you do, not what you say. Time and again, organisations have stated that "people are our greatest asset", then make them redundant. People follow what you do, not what you say. The real company values are shown by who gets rewarded, promoted, or fired. Success needs to be recognised, rewarded, and celebrated to help reinforce desired behaviour.

Always "walk the talk", lead by example and be consistent. Make sure if you ask your team to behave in a certain way that you do it too. Same rules, same values, same behaviours for everyone. Perhaps the worst example I have seen was a director who took delivery of a new company car on the same day that swingeing job cuts were announced.

Finally, in managing and building your teams, there will be times when it just does not seem to be working. Remember to look in the mirror – there is always a possibility that you are the problem. Are they really that bad or have you just been too busy to figure out how to manage and support them?

Your job role is to solve problems and lead change. To work "on" the business, not "in" the business. Sometimes it is just too easy to get caught up in the day to day issues.

4.

How does it all fit together?

The "Business Model" is the blueprint which defines how your business operates and makes money.

Every business contains 9 key parts to their business model covering Customers, Offering, Infrastructure and Financial viability. These are all linked together so if something changes in one part of the model it affects some or all the others.

Since a business invests money in resources and activities to create value & benefits for customers, the model is therefore firmly rooted in the customer and what they need or want:

Customer Segments

Who are you creating value for?

We need to be clear on what an ideal customer looks like so that the rest of the model can be aligned to serving their needs. It is not necessary to create a detailed profile or persona at this stage, just a brief overview of no more than four segments you want to focus on. If you are in B2B include industry sector, company size and job role of decision maker as well.

Value Proposition

What value do they receive?

This is all about what the customer gets out of the relationship. List the problems you are solving for customers, or the needs and wants you are satisfying. We will cover this in more detail in the next section.

Customer Relationships

How do you manage relationship with your customers?

To deliver value to your customers you must manage the relationship with them to achieve sales orders. Relationships may be face to face, virtual, online, telephone, email, via third parties. They may involve lengthy negotiations or maybe just a click. Transactions could be one off or recurring.

Channels & Communications

How do you reach them?

Channels could be physical distribution channels to enable you to physically deliver products or services or channels of communication to enable you to deliver key messages and information to your chosen customer segments.

Revenue Streams

What are the key revenue streams?

Your revenue can be categorised by customer segment, product or service line, geography, or any other way that makes logical sense to your business.

Key Activities

What activities are needed to deliver the value?

To deliver the value outlined in your value proposition there will be specific activities that you need to undertake. These could relate to distribution, sales, marketing, operations, development, research, manufacturing, finance, administration etc.

Key Resources

What resources do you need to deliver the value?

To deliver the value there will be certain resources required in house which will relate to the key activities listed above. These could be people (how many, by function), facilities, equipment, machinery, offices, warehouse etc.

Key Partners

What activities and resources are outsourced?

Partners and suppliers are a fundamental part of most business models where resources and activities are outsourced when it makes commercial sense to do so. As a business evolves and develops, there are phases where outsourcing is the right solution and other phases where bringing skills in house is viable.

Cost Structure

How much does it cost to deliver activities and resources?

Your costs should be broken down into categories for activities and resources and external partners.

Having set out your business model, now challenge it and identify areas for attention:

- What are the key weaknesses or gaps in your current business model?
- What are the key areas which need development?
- What would a competitor need to do to destroy your business?
- If you were starting again as a "new entrant", what would you do differently?
- What are the constraints which hold you back from substantial growth?
- Any other points of vulnerability?

(Tip: The best way to visualise this is to use the Business Model Canvas created by Alexander Osterwalder and Yves Pigneur)

BUSINESS MODEL CANVAS

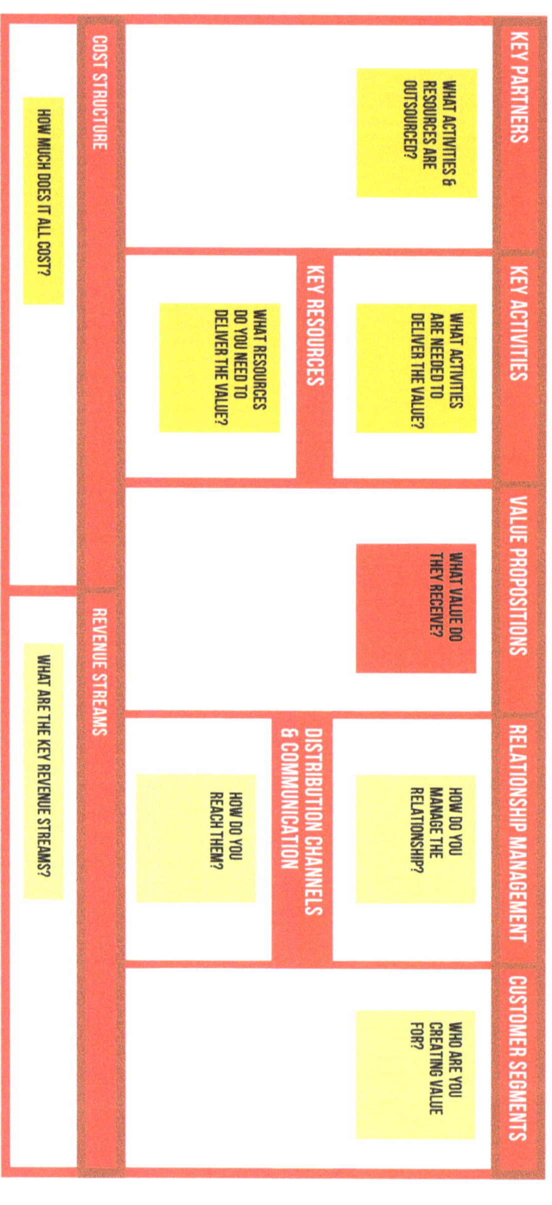

REF: "BUSINESS MODEL GENERATION" BY OSTERWALDER & PIGNEUR

The "What If" game

So now you have an overview of the key components of your business model, we can play the "what if" game.

- What if you set a business goal to grow revenue by 100%, how would this impact on your model?
- This would mean twice as many customers, or the same number of customers buying twice as much or a mix of the two.
- Will these be the same type of customer as today or different one?
- Will these new customers have different requirements which would change your value proposition?
- How will you manage twice as many customer relationships?
- With twice as many customers, what channels would you need to use to reach and service them?
- What additional activities will be required to both service and supply them?
- With twice as many customers how will that impact your level of resources?
- Will you need to outsource more or in source more?
- Finally, what is the impact on the costs of your business? How is this balanced with the increased revenue?

You can apply the "what if" concept to any of the 9 components both positively and negatively to understand the impact, challenges, and risks in each area.

The same structure of the 9 building blocks can be applied to a specific product, division, team or individual. It is really useful for sketching out new product ideas too; this is covered in more detail in the third book in this series (The Business Leaders Essential Guide to Innovation).

5.

What's in it for your customers?

Every business is based on satisfying customer needs and requirements by creating products and services which overcome their pain points or create gains. Customers are not interested in your products or solutions, they are interested in their own problems, challenges, and desires. Your value proposition must align with their agenda, which may also change through time, events, and experience.

The Value Proposition provides a unifying focus for the business by defining the:

- Value delivered
- Problem solved

- Product / Service offered
- Needs or wants satisfied

Let's examine these in more detail:

Customers' purpose

What are the tasks they are trying to perform or fulfil, the problems they are trying to solve, or the needs or wants they are trying to satisfy? When and how do these needs or wants occur? Customers may wish to avoid "pain" or obtain "gain", or both.

Pains

What are the frustrations, fears, needs, negative emotions, undesired costs and situations, risks that your customer experiences in trying to perform the tasks? What worries them or keeps them awake at night? What is stopping them from resolving the problem? What is the overall negative situation they wish to escape from?

Gains

What benefits do your customers expect or desire? What would surprise or delight them? What additional functional utility, social gains, positive emotions, or cost savings do they want? What would make their life easier, fulfil their dreams, make them successful? What is the overall positive impact they desire?

Products / Services

List all your products and services and consider which ones are most closely aligned with your customers pain and gain profiles.

Pain Relievers

How do your products and services remove customer pains?

Gain Creators

How do your products and services deliver customer gains?

The value proposition should ideally focus on a single benefit which is the outcome for the customer. It should be specific, clear, and concise with a sense of urgency. It must mitigate your customers' pain or provide gain.

6.

What are your ambitions?

It is often said the journey is more enjoyable and interesting than reaching the destination. But in business you do need to have a clear focus on what you are trying to achieve, because this in itself will define the nature of the journey. We have already considered the purpose and the principles that will underpin the business. But we need to be also clear on the vision, goals, and ambitions that your plans will be designed to fulfil.

Ambition and vision are often highly personal and will crossover from pure business goals into lifestyle, good causes, personal finance, relationships, and family. So, you should set both personal and business goals. You may not wish to share all your personal goals with your team, but they should certainly be aware that your ambition is bigger than just the business. These goals should be long term and therefore set 3, 5 or even 10 years ahead.

It is a fact of life - at some point you will exit your business. It is preferable from every possible dimension to prepare and plan for this a long time in advance. It may be that you are planning to build your business for sale. If so, you will need an extensive period of preparation to ensure you achieve the best value for your efforts. Specifically, you will need several years of clean and favourable sets of accounts and a credible senior management team to take over from you. In early stage businesses it is often too soon to think about exit plans - so therefore it is best to focus on putting yourself in a position where you have options and alternatives for the next stage of development.

By picking a date in the future, putting a peg in the ground, it becomes possible to work backwards from that date and envisage the key milestones, stages and challenges that will need to be tackled to achieve your goal. Let's focus on what needs to be different to achieve the goal. Just doing the same as before a bit harder will not cut it.

Business Objectives

These tend to be financially orientated (revenue, profit, investment, funding, cash, valuation, share price). They might also include technical developments, market share, new markets, acquisitions - anything which can be quantified and time bound.

Personal Objectives

These can encompass anything from Bucket Lists, Holidays, luxury items such as yachts, cars, or property. It should also include the way you wish to work: the number of days per week, the number of days of holiday, sabbatical periods, retirement plans, other projects, new ventures, and new roles. Do not forget to include friends and family.

Visual Goals

For some, setting out their goals in a visual format such as a mood board, mind map or vision map can be helpful in maintaining focus. A constant reminder on the wall of your office helps keep you going on those days when things or not panning out so well.

Strategic Dimensions

Now that we know the destination that we are aiming for, it is time to consider what that means for each of the core elements of your business. How they will need to evolve and change over time to fulfil your goal, in each case you should define the key milestone stages challenges and events. Inevitably these will interrelate. Significant progress in one dimension will create crisis in another. Therefore, managing the process of growth across all dimensions is crucial to maintain a stable and sustainable growth path. The list below provides a few suggestions on dimensions to consider, and how they will need to evolve:

Financial

What level of sales would you like to achieve in xx years' time?

How big a business do you want to run?

What level of profit would you like to achieve?

What were sales and profit last year?

Customers

How many customers did you have last year? What was their average sale value?

How many customers will you need to have to achieve your long-term sales goal, if their average order stays the same?

How many new customers will you need each year?

How might your new customers be different (bigger, smaller, spend more or less, more or less often …)?

Market Sectors & Geography

What sectors are you currently selling to?

What new sectors might you enter?

Is there sufficient opportunity in your current geographic area or will you need to market in new areas, even new countries?

How will this balance change over time?

Staff

How many people do you currently employ?

How many more will you need and when, to sell and service the business as it grows?

What responsibilities will you need to or want to delegate to others?

What is the average revenue per employee?

What is the average number of customers per employee?

Are you becoming more or less efficient as you grow?

Strategic focus

What is the essential strategic challenge and focus for the business each year, beyond "business as usual"?

Marketing

What is your marketing budget?

What is the key focus of marketing activity today, how will this need to change to provide the leads necessary for your growth?

How many leads do you generate each year and how many convert to sales?

How many more leads, opportunities and orders will you need to fulfil your growth goal?

Products / Services

What are your key products and services - which are the most important contributors to profit?

How will this change over the next 3 years?

Any new products planned?

Channels

How do you currently reach your customer?

Directly or indirectly through distributors or outlets?

What new channels will you require to reach and communicate with new customers?

STRATEGIC DIMENSIONS TABLE

	LAST YEAR	YEAR 1	YEAR 2	YEAR 3
FINANCE SALES (£) PROFIT (£) PROFIT (%)				
CUSTOMERS NUMBER AVERAGE VALUE RETENTION (%) LOST MIX				
STAFF NUMBERS REVENUE PER HEAD NUMBER OF NEW HIRES NEW ROLES				
CHANNELS PARTNERS DISTRIBUTORS MARKETING				
MARKET SECTORS PRIORITY NEW %SPLIT				
GEOGRAPHY				
MARKETING LEADS OPPORTUNITIES RETAINED CUSTOMERS NET NEW CUSTOMERS PRIORITY FOCUS BUDGET				
PRODUCTS & SERVICES CURRENT NEW MIX				
STRATEGIC FOCUS				

Obstacles & Headwinds

In setting out your vision of how the different dimensions unfold into the future it would also be wise to consider what might get in your way. What might be the risks to your plan? So, what are the potential obstacles and headwinds and what can be done to overcome them or weather them?

7.

What are the Key Business Drivers?

There are only 5 ways to grow a business:

Generate more leads
Improve conversation rate of leads into customers
Increase frequency of purchases
Increase value of each purchase
Extend the lifetime of a customer

You and your team need to have clear visibility of your conversion model: how many leads or enquiries do you need to get 1 new "right fit" customer.

You may well define different stages in your conversion model from cold contact to enquiry to lead to opportunity to sale. At each stage you should quantify the ratio. This will drive 2 activities to achieve growth: generating more leads and improving conversion rate of enquiries to orders. This model will define the scale and scope of your marketing to generate more and better converting leads.

Once you have gained a new customer you should consider what could be done to increase their frequency of purchase (gain their repeat orders) and how to increase the value of each purchase by adding in additional options, upgrades or services.

Finally, how can you increase the lifetime value (LTV) of a customer so that they continue to use your products and services for longer. You may need to reconfigure your offering at different stages of a customer's life cycle to ensure you extend your relevance. A proper understanding of a customer's lifetime value is essential in deciding the appropriate level of investment in marketing to gain them. Customer Lifetime Value is one of the most critical measures for any business, yet very few actually record it.

Do not forget to ask your customers – "what would we need to do for you to buy more? or more often, or stay longer? or come back sooner?"

Most customers defect, not because they don't like your product or service but because they feel you are indifferent to them, that you don't care. It also costs far more to gain a new customer than it does to keep an existing one. (Tip: do not be embarrassed to go back to your lapsed customers, they may well regret their decision and be pleased to hear from you)

Remember that if you want to grow your sales you will need to extend activity well outside of the typical first stage customer base of evangelists, innovators, friends, and family. Your next stage customers may well be more demanding and challenging – it is always harder talking to strangers.

Your most loyal, longstanding customers can also be great advocates and ambassadors - but be careful if you let them down, they can also turn into strong detractors.

It is tempting to think that all you need to do to gain new customers is create and publish lots of interesting marketing content. They will enthusiastically consume it, find out about your product or service, and then buy. We live in a content and information rich world; so, it will be crucial to find ways to breakthrough and become visible when we are all overloaded with content already. So, the reality is just inbound & content marketing is rarely enough on its own to develop and grow a business successfully.

It therefore means there will always be an element of cold contact, cold calling, and cold targeting to stimulate and identify new potential customers. The reason why everyone finds cold calling so difficult is deeply embedded in our childhood. Cold calling means talking to strangers, and the one thing our parents told us to do from a very young age was not to talk to strangers!

Your business driver goals should encompass: Customer retention (& growth), New customer acquisition, Lapsed customer recovery and Customer advocacy. It may help to give these themes such as: "Friends & Family", "Talking to Strangers", "Raising the dead", "Loving your fans".

So how do these drivers all fit together, and how do we get from a cold contact to profit:

Let's assume you have built your own list (or acquired a database) of 5000 contacts who match your ideal customer profile. This is cold data, but you have good reason to suspect that these contacts could buy your product. These are just 5000 "Suspects" at this stage.

So now you run a campaign and 10% respond, thereby creating 500 leads ("Prospects"). You run a further campaign to these 500 leads to qualify them and 10% (50) continue to show interest. These 50 can be reasonably classed as Opportunities – they are right fit potential customers. Finally, 20% place an order, giving you 10 new customers.

Each of these customers spends £500 and buys twice in a year generating £10,000 of sales.

Your margin is 30%, therefore you generate £3,000 of profit.

CONVERSION MODEL EXAMPLE

A	COLD CONTACTS			5000
B	CONVERSION RATE	%	10	
C	LEADS	N	A x B% =	500
D	CONVERSION RATE	%	10	
E	OPPORTUNITES	N	C x D% =	50
F	CONVERSION RATE	%	20	
G	CUSTOMERS	N	E x F% =	10
H	NUMBER OF TRANSACTIONS	N	2	
I	AVERAGE SALE PRICE	£	500	
J	TOTAL TURNOVER	£	G x H x I =	10000
K	MARGINS	%	30	
L	PROFIT	£	J x K% =	3000

Conversion Model

So now we know the conversion model:

500 Cold Contacts : 50 Leads : 5 Opportunities : 1 Customer

Therefore, if you want 100 new customers you are going to need to run campaigns to 50,000 contacts, generate 5,000 leads and 500 opportunities.

Improving conversion at each stage has a major impact on profitability and reduces the scale of the lead generation task.

Check Your Lead Process

Please check that your lead process is working correctly on a regular basis. It is surprisingly common for new enquiries to end up in a junk folder, spam filter, an unmonitored email address or messages left are not returned. Automated workflows can get broken inadvertently or through the original architect moving on and no one knowing exactly how it all works.

In a recent mystery shopping test, it was found that only 20% of enquiries were responded to properly, with the majority receiving no response at all.

Speed of response is also essential to improve conversion rates. An enquiry which receives a response within one hour is 80% more likely to convert to a sale.

If your customers first point of contact is through a lead management process which fails, they are unlikely to believe your product is of excellent quality. So, ensure that your lead process is fully documented and checked on a regular basis so that you never risk wasting and neglecting hard won enquiries.

Sales Activity Hours

My client was excitedly sharing his growth plans: 100% over 3 years. I love businesses with ambition and spend much of my time working with them to ensure that their ambition is achieved. This day was no exception. We discussed the resource impact - extra capacity in production, technical, development and a bit of admin all scaled up in line with the growth curve less a little (to allow for some improved efficiency due to scale).

So, what about sales and marketing? I asked. "Oh, we'll probably add in another salesperson and keep marketing the same…." Suddenly we are into "hoping for a miracle" territory.

I checked that 100% growth was the goal, then asked "surely you should be increasing your sales team and marketing resource / budget by 100% also?"

Unless your product or service is so unique that there is unsatisfied demand for it, you are going to need to increase marketing spend to attract interest from new customers; and increase sales resource to convert them to customers. Growth requires investment in the demand end of the process as well as supply. But what is the right level of resource to put into sales?

The proportion of staff resource in sales roles across mid-sized companies is in the range of 10 to 25% of employees. Business at the upper end (25%) seem to be growing faster - yes, the more time and resource you allocate to sales, the more you will sell!!

The challenge for most small or early stage businesses is that no one starts a new business because they love selling. So, achieving growth outside of your existing network means forcing yourself to do something you may not enjoy and do not understand. As a result, sales activity can easily take a lower place in your priority list.

So just a reminder that if you aim to grow, you will need to ensure that you have enough effort, resource and budget for sales and marketing.

The 1% Factor

In some situations, small changes can often have a major impact on profitability. Just a 1 % change can create a surprising improvement. Everyone can make a 1% change surely?

For example, if your margin was 10%, fixed costs 40% and variable costs 50%; reducing your fixed and variable costs by 1%, increasing your price by 1% and selling 1% more would increase profit margin by a staggering 24%.

If that was a 4% change in each, your profit would double.

In the example above, the opposite is also true; a 1% reduction in sales volume and price with a 1% increase in fixed and variable cost will reduce margin by 24%.

Fully understanding the financial drivers of the business is fundamental to appreciate the impact of both favourable and unfavourable changes.

8.

What's most important to work on?

Now we need to focus on the Priority Plans.

What are the three most critical and important priorities which must be addressed? Unless you tackle these three, your growth will not happen, and your business will stagnate.

It is so easy to get caught up in urgent day to day activities, firefighting or crises and find you have not been able to allocate sufficient time to the really important activities. The activities which impact and define the long-term future of the business.

The main difference between an urgent activity and an important activity is that the important ones take longer. So, if you do not start them soon enough your growth plan will forever slip outwards. You have to ensure you spend an increasing amount of time working "on the business", rather than "in the business".

How much time? Well let's start with 20% (1 day a week or 2 half days). Block it off in your diary. If your office is too distracting, work somewhere else. Priorities are priorities.

Priority "Breakthrough" Objectives (What)

So, from all the areas we have explored so far in this book, what are your top three priorities? These are fundamental to enabling or driving growth to achieve your overall aims and goals.

Your three priority objectives could be personal, team, or companywide. They should be inspiring, difficult, and explicit but achievable. You may also choose to set priorities that are stretching and ambitious, or ones that are more readily achieved. After all, once you have achieved one of your objectives you can go on and tackle another one. It is important to focus on just a few priorities, long lists of objectives never get done.

Each of these objectives should begin with the word "To" and should be action orientated. They define "What" you want to achieve: To improve, to increase, to research, to launch, to understand etc

Each one should have a named "Champion" and a target completion date.

Priority Strategies (How)

Then for each of these objectives list four key ways that they will be achieved.

This is the "How". Each of the "Hows" should have an individual named "Owner" and a target completion date. (Tip: Do not allow joint ownership, there needs to be clear responsibility)

So now you have 3 priority objectives for your growth plan each with 4 strategies defining how they will be achieved. That's 12 strategies or projects, and everything is owned and has a deadline.

PRIORITY BREAKTHROUGH PLANS

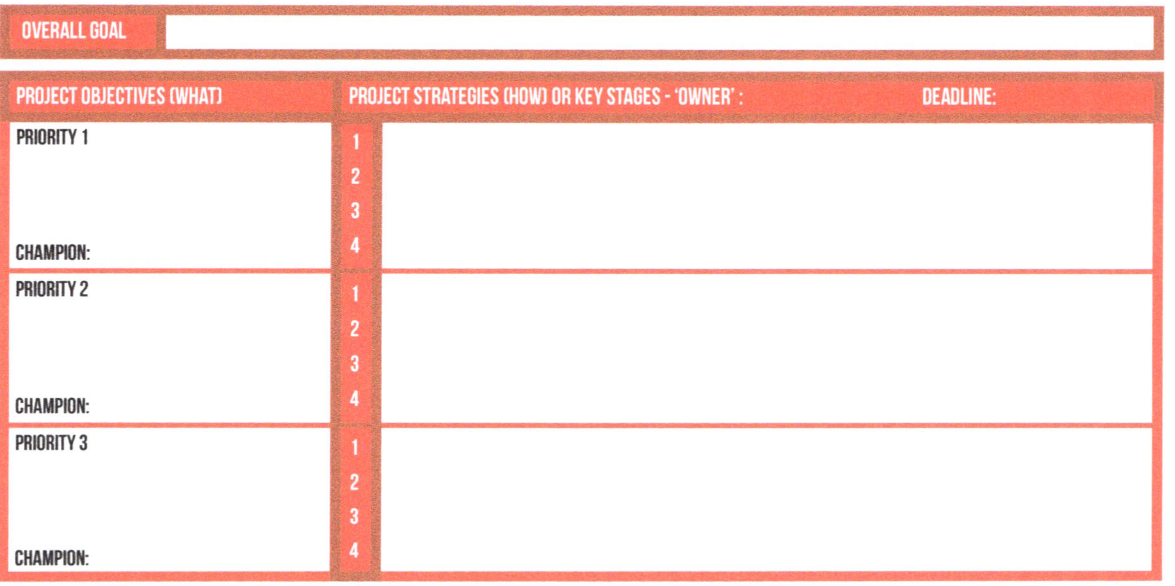

OVERALL GOAL	

PROJECT OBJECTIVES (WHAT)		PROJECT STRATEGIES (HOW) OR KEY STAGES - 'OWNER' :	DEADLINE:
PRIORITY 1	1		
	2		
	3		
CHAMPION:	4		
PRIORITY 2	1		
	2		
	3		
CHAMPION:	4		
PRIORITY 3	1		
	2		
	3		
CHAMPION:	4		

Publish & Share.

Now publish and share these with the whole team. This ensures that everyone is aware of the key priorities, can therefore align their own activities and contribute their own ideas to help. It means that anyone can ask any champion or strategy owner about how they are getting on. Publicly publishing ensures visibility for everyone and applies a crucial layer of peer pressure to ensure that these things do get done. The best way to publish and share is the most visible, so stick them on the wall where everyone can see them.

KPIS – "Weighing a pig every day doesn't make it get fatter"

Monitoring progress on a regular basis with these priority plans is critically important to ensure that the activities are prioritised. Anything that moves off track should instigate a corrective action. One of the most common ways of keeping an eye on progress is through key performance indicators (KPIs). These are key objective measures to enable you to monitor progress.

However, it is important not to confuse "reporting" with KPIs. It is not the measure itself, it's what it means and what you do about it that counts.

KPIs need to be KEY, stretch beyond "Business as Usual" and lead to action.

They need to be focused on improving performance and achieving the result, not just maintaining it. Ben Hunt-Davis and Harriet Beveridge captured this rather well in their book "Will it make the boat go faster". This was the mantra which the 2000 Olympic Gold medal rowing team used as their KPI for everything - nutrition, training, clothing, tactics. If it didn't make the boat go faster, they didn't do it.

To be effective KPIs should be agreed for everyone (yes, even you). They should be shared openly and transparently, so that everyone can understand and see what each team is striving for, and how achieving their own KPIs meshes in with others. Setting and imposing KPIs will not overcome poor leadership or management.

To achieve genuine performance improvement Key Performance Indicators can exist at different levels: Activity, Impact, Outcome, Process, Finance or Conversion level.

Activity level (self-measure)

These are day to day parameters which an individual will use to manage their own focus, priority, and performance. They have no direct impact on others. They do not need to be reported on. Management should only be interested in confirming that individuals are setting their own Activity Measures, measuring their own success, and adjusting activity accordingly.

Impact level (lead measure)

These are the tangible impacts or effects of the individual activities above. They may have impact on others. Management should be aware of these and be interested in these measures.

Output level (lag measure)

These are the key business drivers. They are the desired output, effect, and outcome of activities. Management should be fully aware of these and seeking improvement at every opportunity.

Process level (ratios)

These are performance ratios that record stages in processes. They may exist within a team or between teams. They are ideal for real time dashboards, so long as they tie into actions (corrective or celebratory).

Finance level (ratios)

These are largely backward looking and measure key financial trends. They should also be projected forward into forecasts to alert to risk and exposure.

Conversion Model (Ratio)

These are the activity or action steps leading to gaining a new customer, regaining a lapsed customer, or securing a repeat customer as shown in the previous chapter.

So What?

With any measure, data, analysis, or report, always ask yourself the "So What" question. Every report or analysis should have a conclusion and recommendations for action.

If the goal is to achieve growth, everyone needs to be fully engaged with the process and play their part irrespective of their seniority or role.

The 4F Framework for Problem Solving

Inevitably not everything will go according to plan. There may be unforeseen events or obstacles that could not have been foreseen. Your role as a business leader is to solve problems and manage change but it's often easy to be discouraged and distracted when things don't go right.

The 4F framework is designed for those situations, to steer and guide your thinking to productive solutions. A further book in this series will focus on innovation tools and techniques where significant new thinking is required.

Frame

Step back from the issue and think cleanly. What is the real issue here? Are you trying to solve a symptom without recognising the underlying disease? What is the real narrative behind the problem? How can you change your perception or your attitude to it? Ultimately how can you reframe or redefine the problem? Too often we leap in and end up trying to solve the wrong problem and miss the root cause.

Focus

Where are you going to focus? Ignore what you cannot change and focus solely on what you can change. What do you need to have, not what would be nice to have?

Force

What effort needs to be applied to this? What resources, time and money are required? What is the impact of diverting resources or delay? How hard will you need to push? Can the team step up a gear?

Flow

Envisage what the future state will look like when this problem is resolved, and the plan is back on track. In resolving this the team may establish a different level of flow, the point at which everything is flowing smoothly. Along the way where will you experience fear and find excitement? How can you make this situation enjoyable for all? How can you channel this experience to energise and motivate? What will you learn from it? How can you make solving problems fun?

4F FRAMEWORK

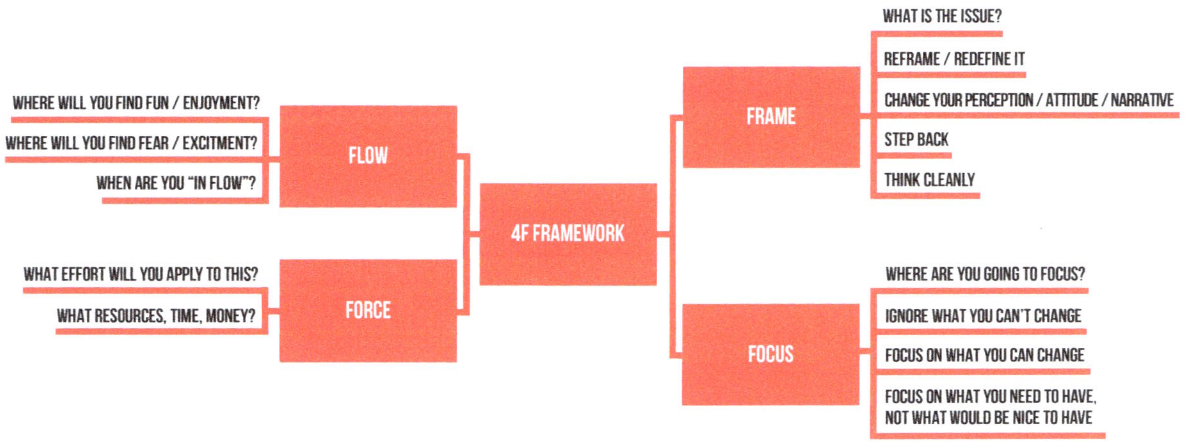

9.

What are the specific activities and tasks?

Each one of your 12 priority strategies now need to have its own detailed action plan.

It should be the responsibility of the strategy owner to set out this plan, to update it based on progress, and to ensure the status is published and visible for all to see. They should also propose corrective action.

The strategy owner should report to the priority objective champion who in turn reports to the board or managing director. This way responsibility is firmly delegated and spread throughout the team. (TIP: the managing director, founder or business owner should not own any of the strategies)

One Page Plans

A simple One Page Plan format is ideal for this, created in Excel.

List the major stages or action steps to whatever level of detail is appropriate to the task. For each stage specify: **what** it is, **how** it will be done, **when** it will be done by (date), **who** will be doing it (responsibility), how you will know it has been completed (measurable), progress (status) and a column for comments.

The progress column should be categorised by status and colour:

Red	Off target, action required
Amber	In progress, not on target
Green	In progress, on target
White	Not started, scheduled later

The plan should be updated constantly and published by a set time each week (e.g. 14:00 every Friday).

This approach removes the need for update meetings to report on progress since that is self-evident from the document. It also means that the only items worthy of serious discussion are the red items which are off target and require action.

It always helps to get a plan down to a single page, as this significantly increases the likelihood of it being fulfilled.

Project Management Plans

For more complex projects it is wise to undertake a more detailed project planning process. Use one of the many project management platforms to ensure that the project is broken down into appropriate stages, and that visibility is maintained on progress. These platforms also make it easier to manage projects with multiple partners in different locations without the need for lengthy time-wasting meetings.

10.

How are you going to schedule and ensure delivery?

Most growth plans stall not because they are bad plans or because the objectives, goals and strategies are ill conceived. They fail because of a lack of interest or the discipline required for the sheer grind involved in making things happen.

Many organisations run annual strategy days or away days to brainstorm new ideas. Sadly, by the time the event come round the next year little has changed, and cynicism quickly sets in. Maybe running a regular Tactics & Action Planning session would be more worthwhile.

Whilst the goal remains the same, what you do to deliver on it will change. The tactics must change and evolve in response to Increased knowledge, Validation of assumptions, Success or Failure of actions, External events – markets, competitors, politics, economy

The real competitive edge for most market leaders is not the brilliance of their creativity, technology, innovation, and strategy. Indeed, many do not have the best product or the best service. But what they do have is the instinct, energy, drive, discipline, and commitment to implement.

How do we fix this?

The OOOO Model – how to make it happen

This framework tackles the issues of task ownership, clear objectives, focus on outcomes, and the need to be held to account.

Ownership

If no one owns it, it's no one's responsibility
if no one is responsible, no one cares
If no one cares, it's no one's priority
if it's no one's priority, it slips to the bottom of the To Do List
If it's at the bottom of the To Do List, it won't get done

Every part of the plan needs to have a single individual's name against it. Someone who owns it, is committed to it, feels responsible and will feel recognised when they deliver. Never allow joint ownership of a strategy or task – joint ownership guarantees inefficiency and risks the critical task falling into the gap between the joint owners. Don't neglect to ensure that these tasks are included in appraisals and personal objectives. Your team needs to know this is serious not an optional add on task.

Objectives

Knowing what you are aiming at is essential to enable the team to focus and keep the purpose in mind. Clearly defined goals provide a reference point which enables everyone to filter out activities which do not align to the goal. This should also empower everyone in the team to question any activity which does not move the project forward. It is not unusual for the busines owner to also be the most disruptive force. So, empowering your team to hold you to account also can be beneficial (if uncomfortable). Entrepreneurs have a habit of constantly thinking of new ideas, which they share with their team. The same team that is still wrestling to implement yesterday's great idea. So, yesterday's idea never gets finished and the team is confused, unproductive and demotivated. (Tip: keep a log of new ideas, reflect on them before sharing and have a category called "Next Year")

Objectives should clearly define what is going to be different at the target date. This should be expanded so that the future state is more than a number, with some qualitative elements too. We have discussed business goals and your personal goals earlier; do not forget the personal goals for the team and how this plan will help achieve their aspirations too.

Outcomes

Whilst the overall objective is the goal, each stage in the plan will have its own outcomes which feed into other stages. Delay in any one stage will impact on subsequent stages. Therefore, the plan must have many defined results and milestones. This way you can be sure it stays on track and you can take early corrective action if any stage stalls. What is measured gets done, so it is essential that everyone commits to the outcomes to be achieved. As always publish them and make them visible for all to see. If you are using the traffic light system outlined above, a weekly update on the whiteboard of how many tasks are Red, Amber or Green can provide a very simple visual prompt for all to see. Alternatively, you can establish more complex stages showing tasks which are Live, Stalled, On Hold, Awaiting Brief, New, Complete, In Progress etc.

Ouch

Ultimately, every member of your team including yourself needs to be held to account to ensure key deadlines are met and that the desired pace of progress is achieved. One of the joys of being a business owner is that as you are your own boss, so it's down to you to hold yourself to account - or to give your team permission to do so. So, we need some pressure and may be bit of pain to make things happen.

How are you going to schedule and ensure delivery?

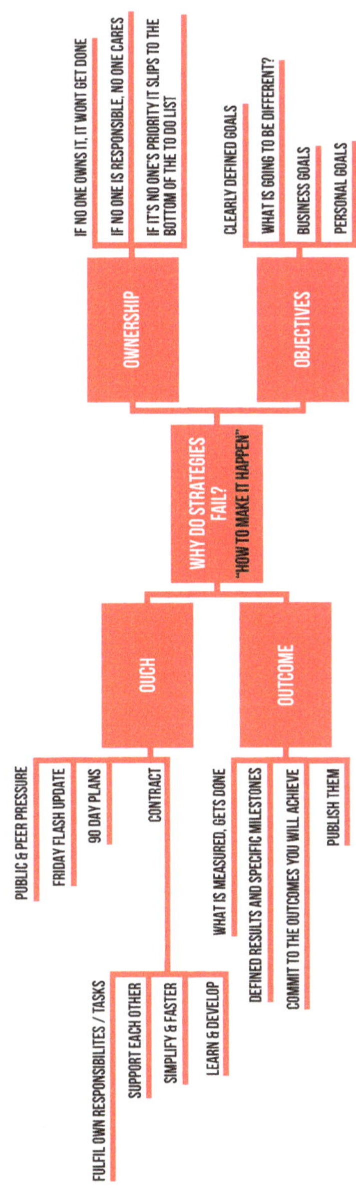

Contract

Set out a written "contract" or "charter" with your team agreeing to fulfil their own responsibilities and tasks. Within this, commit to supporting each other, finding simpler and faster methods at every opportunity. Treat every stage as an opportunity to learn, develop and share to improve team capability.

90-day plans

Break the plan down into 90-day sprints, its far easier to focus on what will be delivered in shorter timescales.

Flash update reports

Weekly updates on this week's progress and next week's actions from all team members is great way to end a week. Just a simple email with a list of the key actions completed this week and the key action plan for next week. This ensures that Monday can kick off straight away without timewasting updates sessions. Everyone is then aware of pressure points and can help if need be. Plus, it adds in the constant public and peer pressure to help push everyone along.

11.

What's going to get in your way?

Here are 15 barriers which can hold you back.

Not having a goal

"if you don't know where you are going, any road leads there" Lewis Carroll

Expecting a smooth ride

The goal remains the same, what you do to deliver on it will change

"No battle plan ever survives contact with the enemy" Helmuth von Moltke the Elder

"Management practices that work well in one phase may bring on a crisis in another." Larry Greiner

The wrong people

Trying to work with the wrong Team, Customers, Partners, Collaborators, Suppliers.

Only work with people you enjoy working and spending time with.

"Nothing will kill a great employee faster than watching you tolerate a bad one " Perry Belcher

Self-Deception / Self Discipline

How much time are you actually working?

Are you really pushing hard ahead?

Is what you are doing making money, spending it or wasting money?

"If you think you can do a thing or think you can't do a thing, you're right". Henry Ford

Perfectionism

Perfectionism + Procrastination = Paralysis

80% is good enough for 80% of situations 80% of the time

"Done is better than perfect" Sheryl Sandberg

"A good plan today is better than a perfect one tomorrow" General George Patton

Procrastination

Just do it (JFDI)

"Action without vision is only passing time, vision without action is merely daydreaming; but vision with action can change the world" Nelson Mandela

It is delivery that matters

"Your customers don't care how hard you tried; they measure you on what you deliver" Steve Jobs

Urgent v Important

Important things take longer

Do it now, Delegate it, Schedule it or Delete it (The Eisenhower Matrix)

If in doubt, follow the money

"I have two kinds of problems, the urgent and the important. The urgent are not important, and the important are never urgent." President Dwight D Eisenhower

Personal productivity

Harness technology, visual tools, schedule time, prioritise & focus hard, but ensure you take care of body, health, mind, and self.

"The secret to getting things done is to ACT." Dante

Trying to do it all yourself

The impossible job description of a business founder: sales, procurement, operations, marketing, accounts, debt collection, recruitment, fund raising, legal, office admin, strategy, personal assistant, public relations, manager, trainer, customer care, research, development.

"Only do what only you can do." Sir John Harvey Jones

Blaming others

If you want to know why your business is not growing – always look in the mirror first.

"Your company's employees practice the behaviours that are valued, not the values you believe." Dr Cameron Sepah

Driving with the brake on

"making the boat go slower"
If it does not contribute to the strategy and help achieve the goal – DON'T DO IT

Measuring everything

Analysis paralysis, too much data, too many reports.

"It is wrong to suppose that if you can't measure it, you can't manage it – a costly myth." W. Edwards Deming

All talk, no action

"The way to get started is to quit talking and start doing." Walt Disney

Tolerating Unacceptable behaviour

"If we accept behaviour that's unacceptable, we're compromising on something that we thought was too important to compromise on. And that's how we end up with the unacceptable becoming commonplace." Seth Godin

Trying to keep everyone happy

"If you want to make everyone happy, don't be a leader. Sell Ice Cream." Steve Jobs
"Remember if growing a business was easy everyone would be doing it." Stephen Dann

12.

Recommended Reading

The Business Leaders Essential Guide to Marketing
Stephen Dann

The Business Leaders Essential Guide to Innovation
Stephen Dann

The One Minute Manager
Ken Blanchard and Spencer Johnson

Eat That Frog
Brian Tracy

Who Moved my Cheese?
Spencer Johnson

Pig Wrestling
Peter Lindsay and Mark Bawden

Managing Difficult People
David Cotton

Fish
Stephen C Lundin, Harry Paul, and John Christensen

Your Best Year Yet
Jinny Ditzler

The Five Dysfunctions of a Team
Patrick Lencioni

Business Model Generation
Alexander Osterwalder and Ives Pigneur

Start with Why
Simon Sinek

Leaders Eat Last
Simon Sinek

Will it make the boat go faster?
Ben Hunt-Davis and Harriet Beveridge

Measure What Matters
John Doeer

Business Models for Teams
Tim Clark, Bruce Hazen, and Yves Pigneur

High Output Management
Andy Grove

Who Not How
Dan Sullivan with Dr Benjamin Hardy

About the Author

Stephen Dann is a creative thinker, innovator, marketer, strategist, author, and renowned business adviser.

He has built and led marketing teams in 5 major organisations building high performing teams, harnessing new technology and innovative approaches. Leaving corporate life behind, he developed a series of small and medium sized enterprises and fully experienced the highs and lows of the entrepreneurial journey.

He founded Business Impact Solutions Ltd in 2005 specifically to help business leaders and entrepreneurs tackle the challenges of growth, marketing, and innovation. As a business, management, and marketing consultant he has worked with over 400 client companies to date, ranging from mature global corporates and not for profit organisations to SMEs and high growth early-stage businesses across a wide range of sectors. He is a registered expert for the European Commission and is regularly called on to advise on the commercialisation of ground-breaking innovation.

Stephen is passionate about innovation, creativity, and change. He is recognised for seeking new ideas and insights to help businesses solve their commercial problems through creative and imaginative use of technology and marketing.

He believes that organisations only truly fulfil their potential and achieve their goals if they change the way they behave, change the way they operate or change some other fundamental aspect of the business. He constantly reminds business leaders that doing what you have always done and just exhorting teams to work harder is the best way to ensure those goals are not achieved.

Stephen is dedicated to helping businesses fix the problems that prevent organisations, teams, and individuals from achieving their potential.

As a sought-after business coach, consultant, and speaker, Stephen openly shares his tried, tested, and innovative approaches with entrepreneurs, business leaders and their teams.

Information on Stephen's books, insights and other materials can be found at:

www.businessimpactsolutions.co.uk

www.ingramcontent.com/pod-product-compliance
Lightning Source LLC
Chambersburg PA
CBHW040928210326
41597CB00030B/5224

* 9 7 8 1 7 3 9 9 7 9 8 0 5 *